Handmade
Fairy Cards

Judy Balchin

SEARCH PRESS

First published in Great Britain 2008

Search Press Limited
Wellwood, North Farm Road,
Tunbridge Wells, Kent TN2 3DR

Text copyright © Judy Balchin 2008

Photographs by Debbie Patterson at Search Press studios

Photographs and design copyright © Search Press Ltd 2008

ISBN: 978-1-84448-305-1

The Publishers and author can accept no responsibility for any consequences arising from the information, advice or instructions given in this publication.

Readers are permitted to reproduce any of the items in this book for their personal use, or for the purposes of selling for charity, free of charge and without the prior permission of the Publishers. Any use of the items for commercial purposes is not permitted without the prior permission of the Publishers.

Suppliers

If you have difficulty in obtaining any of the materials and equipment mentioned in this book, then please visit the Search Press website for details of suppliers: www.searchpress.com

Publisher's note

All the step-by-step photographs in this book feature the author, Judy Balchin, demonstrating how to make fairy greetings cards. No models have been used.

Printed in Malaysia

Dedication

To Debbie Smith
… and your wicked sense of humour. Thank you!

Acknowledgements

Once again, a huge thank you to all the lovely team at Search Press… I almost feel like 'one of the family' now! In particular Roz Dace for her continued support and encouragement, Edd the editor for his sense of fun and unerring belief in my talent, Ellie Burgess for her wonderful design skills and Debbie Patterson for her stylish photography.
Thank you too to John Wright of Pebeo UK for providing the glass-painting materials used in this book. A big thank you to Joanna Sheen for letting me use her *Victorian Angels and Fairies* CD-ROM, (www.joannasheen.com) to create the images for the shaker cards.
Also to Personal Impressions, Penny Black, Funstamps, Sirius Hobby and Hero Arts (© 2007 Hero Arts, all rights reserved), for giving me permission to use their rubber stamps to which they hold copyright.

Cover: Flower Fairy
This vibrant glass-painted fairy is backed with starry holographic card to give her that extra magic sparkle.

Page 1: Forget-me-not Fairy
A dark blue base card and coloured glitter papers are used as a background for this cute polymer clay fairy, giving it a funky twist.

Contents

Introduction

I have literally been 'away with the fairies' for the duration of writing this book and have enjoyed every magical minute of it. The end of every day has found me covered in glitter and usually sporting a few gold and silver sequins as I wander round my local supermarket. This has naturally raised a few comments amongst my friends and family. So at last, here it is: my lovely book of fairy cards. Having had such a wonderful time creating my magical friends, I found it quite sad when the last card was finally completed; but the thought of all you fairy enthusiasts reading this and being enticed into my enchanted world, soon brought a big smile back to my face.

You will be invited to meet all my magical friends as you work your way through the projects in the book. Greet Funky Fairy and have fun creating her robe and headdress using all those crafty sequins, beads and buttons that you have stored away in your craft cupboard. Discover the art of making a shaker card with the ethereal Snow Fairy. Flower Fairy can not wait to be transformed with vibrant glass paints and Fun Fairy is dying to be created from colourful polymer clay. Forest Fairy is patiently waiting on page 34, ready to be 'stamped' into life and finally, Frost Fairy is beginning to stamp her tiny icy foot – have a go at some enchanted foil embossing! Oh, and do not forget to visit their friends on the variations pages after each project.

The fairies have all faithfully promised to cast their tiny spells as you work. I hope that by the time you have finished making the cards in the book you too will be away with the fairies... and be proud of it! Have fun,

Judy

A small selection of the cards illustrated in this book.

Materials

All of the projects featured in this book are created using materials that can be found easily in art and craft shops.

Basic materials

You will not need all of the items listed in the following pages for the projects. Each project provides you with a specific materials list for you to look at before you begin.

Pencil Use this to draw lines and to trace templates.

Ruler Use a ruler to measure and draw straight lines. It is also used with the back of a scalpel to score a fold line in card.

Scalpel Use this for cutting card. Use the back of the scalpel to score fold lines in card.

Cutting mat Cut card and paper with a scalpel on this.

Scissors Round-ended scissors are used for cutting paper and card.

Old scissors These are used for cutting wire and embossing foil.

Spray glue This is used to glue background paper and acetate on to card.

Crafter's glue Use this to attach gems, sequins and fabric flowers to card.

Strong clear adhesive Use this to glue embossing foil to card.

Masking tape Secure acetate with this before painting. Use for securing a template to foil before embossing.

Double-sided sticky pads Sticky pads are used to attach card shapes to the base card to give a three-dimensional effect.

Round paintbrush A soft synthetic brush is used for glass painting.

Flat paintbrush This is used to paint pieces of card with acrylic paint.

Large soft paintbrush Use this to brush excess glitter from your cards.

Clay shaper This is used to join two pieces of polymer clay together.

Palette Mix glass paints with clear medium on a palette.

Old pad Use this as a padded surface when embossing foil.

Scrap paper Work over this when using glitter.

White ceramic tile Work on this to create your polymer clay fairies.

Embossing tool This is used to create the eyes and mouth of the polymer clay fairy, but it is also useful for metal embossing.

Ballpoint pen This is useful for embossing foil if you can not find your embossing tool!

Paper and card

A huge choice of backing papers and card is now available from art and craft shops. The selection shown here includes assorted coloured card and papers, patterned background papers, handmade papers, corrugated card, holographic and glitter card, metallic and mirror card and embossing foils.

I have also used images printed from Joanna Sheen's *Victorian Angels and Fairies* CD in the shaker card project on pages 16–21.

Joanna Sheen's CD and some images printed from it.

Embellishments

Ribbons, embroidery cottons, gems, sequins, buttons, beads, wire, fabric flowers... all can be used to decorate your cards. Glitter is used to create the sparkly backgrounds of the glass-painted cards.

Polymer clay, roller and cutters

Polymer clay is used to create the Fun Fairy (see pages 28–31). Cutters are used to cut out polymer clay shapes after being rolled with a rolling pin or small plastic tube. Keep some baby wipes nearby to clean your hands and rolling pin when using coloured polymer clay.

Acrylic paints, glass paints, outliners and acetate

Acrylic paints are used to decorate the card panels on pages 34–37. Glass paints, outliners and acetate are used to create the cards on pages 22–25.

Black outliner is used for outlining the design on to acetate. When glass-painting a design on to acetate to use in your cardmaking, you will find it necessary to dilute some of the darker paints with the clear glass-painting medium to give a lighter, more pastel look. Glass paints used straight from the bottle can appear rather dark.

Solvent-based clear glass-painting varnish is used for the background on the Frost Fairy (see pages 40–43).

Rubber stamps, embossing pads and inkpads, coloured pencils and felt-tip pens

Keep a look out for fairy themed rubber stamps and background stamps at your local art and craft shops. An embossing pad and powders are used in stamp embossing work, along with a heat tool.

In the Forest Fairy project (see pages 34–37), a black inkpad is used to stamp the basic fairy. Coloured pencils are also used in this project. Felt-tip pens are used to colour a stamp and to create the facial features of the Funky Fairy and her friends (see pages 10–15).

Foam tape

This is used to create the raised frame of the Snow Fairy (see pages 16–19) and the other shaker cards on pages 20–21.

Funky Fairy

Perhaps we should re-name this Funky Fairy 'Bits and Bobs' as that is exactly what she is made of! For this project you will be definitely be searching through your boxes of crafty goodies looking for sequins, beads and buttons – anything shiny and glitzy, in fact. Make sure that you use a good thick card when creating the robe as thinner card may warp.

YOU WILL NEED

White card measuring 10 x 17cm (4 x 6¾in) when folded in half

Lilac card: 7 x 14cm (2¾ x 5½in)

Spotted pink background paper: 9 x 16cm (3½ x 6¼in)

White and pink card

Pink sparkly paper

Coloured sequins and small beads

Pink buttons

Silver wire

Sparkly white embroidery thread

Red and black fine felt-tip pens

Double-sided sticky pads

Crafter's glue

Spray glue

Scalpel

Ruler

Paintbrush

The templates for the Funky Fairy card, reproduced at actual size.

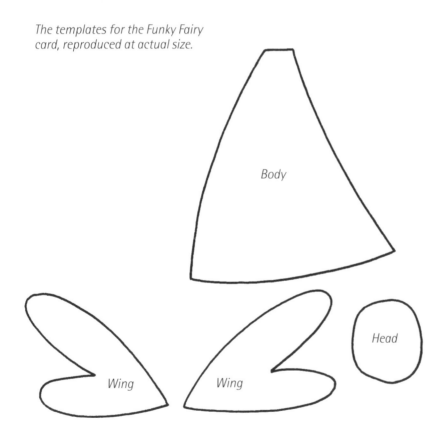

Body

Wing

Wing

Head

Opposite:
The finished card. Create a matching gift tag using the same glitzy papers and sequins as the card.

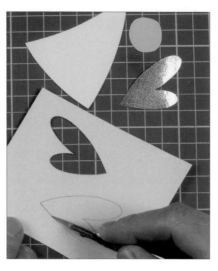

1 Use spray glue to attach the spotted paper to the card base and the lilac card on top.

2 Using the templates to help you, cut the fairy's body from white card, the head from pink card and the wings from pink sparkly paper.

Tip

It is easier to transfer your pattern to the back of the sparkly paper.

3 Squeeze crafter's glue over the card body shape a little at a time and drop coloured sequins and beads on to it. Position them with the tip of a paintbrush (see inset). Completely cover the body shape.

Tip

Use a damp paintbrush to pick up the sequins.

4 When the sequined body has dried, use crafter's glue to attach the sparkly wings to the back of the body.

5 Glue sequins and beads around the top of the head shape and when dry, draw in the eyes and mouth with the felt-tip pens.

6 Attach a sticky pad to the back of the head and remove the backing paper.

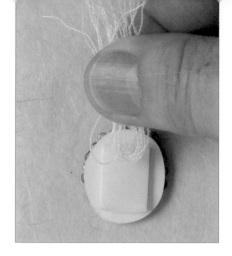

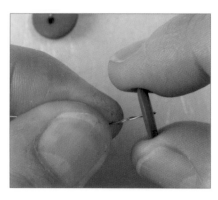

7 Cut a few 10cm (4in) lengths of sparkly white embroidery cotton. Fold the lengths in half and press the folds on to the sticky pads so that the threads splay out to create the hair.

8 Cut two lengths of wire for the legs. Thread a button on to each length and twist the wires to secure the button. Trim each leg to 8cm (3in) long.

9 Attach the wire ends to the back of the body with sticky pads.

10 Peel off the backing papers and press the body on to the base card.

11 Press the head above the body so that it overlaps the body slightly.

Funky Fairy is now waiting to create a little magic.

Christmas Fairy

This simple Christmas tree is crowned with a glitzy gold fairy. Use gold sequins and beads and silver stars to decorate her festive frock and hat. Gold wire arms threaded with a heart button make her the perfect fairy card to send to your loved one. The matching gift tag uses a heart motif to continue the loving theme.

Moon Fairy

Silver gems, sequins and beads are used to help this moon fairy fly into orbit! For extra sparkle, her legs and arms are created with silver glitter wire and her wings from glitter card. Our fairy is backed with silver mirror card and heart background paper to make a truly magical creation.

Dragonfly Fairy

The background dragonfly paper is the inspiration for this fairy. Green and blue sequins and beads are used to decorate her headdress and robe. Green wire and buttons make the legs and her wings are cut from iridescent green paper. A matching gift tag is decorated with buttons and sequins.

Snow Fairy

Bring this thoughtful Snow Fairy to life by including icy silver sequins and stars into the central shaker panel. All the images in this section are printed from a CD on a computer. They are supplied in different sizes to give you a choice as to the size of your card. Cool colours are used to reflect the beauty of her frozen world.

YOU WILL NEED

Fairy images taken from Joanna Sheen's *Victorian Angels and Fairies* CD

Lilac card measuring 13 x 15cm (5 x 6in) when folded in half

Pale blue glitter card: 12 x 14.5cm (4¾ x 5¾in) and 8 x 10.5cm (3 x 4in)

Rainbow card 11 x 13.5cm (4¼ x 5¼in)

White card 8 x 10.5cm (3 x 4in)

Acetate 7 x 9.5cm (2¾ x 3¾in)

Sticky foam tape

Silver star gems and sequins

Irridescent sequins

Pale blue organza ribbon

Scalpel

Ruler

Spray glue

Crafter's glue

Computer

1   Use spray glue to attach the larger piece of pale blue glitter card to the base card and the rainbow card on top.

2   Print out the 6 x 8.5cm (2¼ x 3¼in) fairy image on your computer and cut it out. Glue it to the middle of the piece of white card with crafter's glue.

Opposite:
The finished card. Print a smaller fairy image from the CD to use on a matching gift tag.

3 Press lengths of foam tape round the white border, trimming them neatly to fit.

4 Place the gems and sequins within the recess and gently remove the backing tape on the foam strips.

Tip

Always place your sequins into the recess before you remove the backing papers.

5 Press the acetate on to the foam frame.

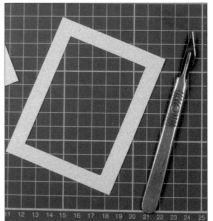

6 Measure and draw a 1cm (½in) border on to the back of the smaller piece of pale blue glitter card. Cut out the aperture using the scalpel.

7   Press the glitter card frame on top of the acetate.

8   Glue the shaker panel to the middle of the base card with crafter's glue.

9   Use crafter's glue to attach a ribbon bow to the top left corner of the frame.

10   Decorate the card with stars.

Your finished Snow Fairy, surrounded by her icy embellishments.

Nature Fairy

Gold and silver sequin stars and leaves are inserted into this shaker card to mirror this Nature Fairy as she listens to the birds. The frame is decorated with flower sequins and gems and a backing panel of floral paper echoes the theme. The simple matching gift tag uses just one flower embellishment as a central motif.

Dream Fairy

Blue and silver sets the theme for this Dream Fairy as she sits watching the moonlit sea. The shaker panel uses small blue and silver sequins as decoration with a surrounding frame of glitter card. Backed with a panel of torn handmade paper and decorated with a sprinkling of tiny stars, this card will make sure that this fairy's dreams will come true. The matching gift tag uses a smaller picture version of the main card. This is also provided on the CD.

Frolicking Fairies

Iridescent and pastel glitter papers are used to mirror this delicate picture of Frolicking Fairies. Sparkling stars dance in the shaker panel as the fairies swoop and dive.

Flower Fairy

Create a little magic by using diluted glass paints to bring this vibrant Flower Fairy to life. Glass painting has always been my therapy, so get out those outliners and glass paints and enjoy the journey with me. She is backed with a starry sky of holographic card to give her that extra sparkle and sits delicately against a rainbow surround. Always apply glass paint generously.

YOU WILL NEED

White base card measuring
11.5 x 19cm (4½ x 7½in) when
folded in half

Thick card 14 x 21cm (5½ x 8¼in)

Rainbow background paper
11.5 x 19cm (4½ x 7½in)

Silver star holographic card
12 x 20cm (4¾ x 7¾in)

Acetate

Black outliner

Glass paints: red, light yellow, deep
yellow, turquoise

Glass-painting gloss medium

Fabric flowers

Paintbrush

Palette

Masking tape

Spray glue

Scissors

Scalpel

Ruler

The templates for the Flower Fairy card and tag, reproduced at three-quarters of the actual size. You will need to photocopy each at 133 per cent for the correct size.

Opposite:
The butterfly template used on the tag complements the finished card beautifully.

1 Photocopy the template, cut round it using the scalpel and ruler, then tape it to a piece of thick card. Tape a slightly larger piece of acetate over the top.

Tip
Dilute each glass paint with gloss medium to give a more pastel appearance to the fairy.

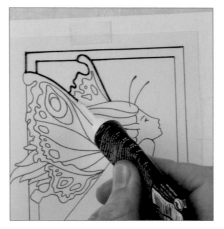

2 Use the tube of outliner to outline the design. Leave to dry and remove the template.

3 Mix a drop of red and yellow glass paints with gloss medium in a palette to create a flesh tone. Paint the fairy's skin.

4 Paint the hair with diluted light yellow and the dress with diluted deep yellow.

5 Paint the wings with diluted red and yellow paints adding undiluted spots of red.

6 Fill in the branch, small flower and outer border with red glass paint.

7   Mix up a good quantity of diluted turquoise glass paint in a palette and fill in the background. Leave to dry.

8   Cut out the acetate fairy with scissors. Spray the back of the acetate with spray glue and press it on to silver holographic card. Cut it out with scissors (see inset).

9   Cover the front of the base card with rainbow background paper. Use spray glue to attach the fairy to the middle of the base card.

10   Decorate the fairy and the card with fabric flowers, attaching them with crafter's glue.

Flower Fairy can not wait to fly off and visit family and friends!

Fairy Queen

This glass-painted image is mounted on to starry holographic card. The cut-out image is then backed with a panel of glitter card. Small silver stars, gems and fabric flowers are used to bring this fairy to life. The matching gift tag uses a small glass-painted butterfly as its central image.

Toadstool Fairy

This delicate Toadstool Fairy is painted on to acetate and mounted on to mirror card. The cut-out image is then backed with a vibrant red card panel and holographic card. Small red floral gems are used to mirror the colour of the vibrant toadstool.

Love Fairy

Cards are made and sent with love. This Love Fairy card uses vibrant glass paints to send its cheery message. Sparkling paper and mirror card back the central image. For that extra twinkle small gems are used as embellishments. The butterfly gift tag uses the same basic coloured paints as the main card.

Fun Fairy

Polymer clay is great fun to use. Fun Fairy cried out to be created with bright colours and glittery wings and here she is! Make sure that you clean your rolling pin and hands between each clay colour so that you do not contaminate them. Working on a ceramic tile means that, once created, she can be slipped easily into the oven for baking.

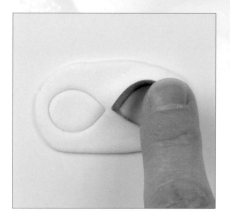

1   Working on a white tile, roll out a small amount of white glitter clay, and use the leaf cutter to cut two leaf shapes for the wings.

Tip

Make sure that you keep your hands and equipment clean at all times. Use baby wipes to clean your hands and roller between colours.

YOU WILL NEED

Orange base card measuring 11 x 14cm (4⁹/₁₂ x 5¹/₂in) when folded in half

Patterned glitter card 10 x 13cm (4 x 5¹/₄in)

Yellow card 4.5 x 9cm (1³/₄ x 3¹/₂in)

Polymer clay: white with glitter, flesh coloured, mandarin orange and lime green

White ceramic tile

Rolling pin

Small leaf and flower cutters

Scroll-patterned rubber stamp: Penny Black 2636K

Dot-patterned rubber stamp: Hero Arts LL848 (part of an assorted patterns pack)

Embossing tool

Clay shaper

Double-sided sticky pads

Strong clear glue

Scalpel

Ruler

Baby wipes

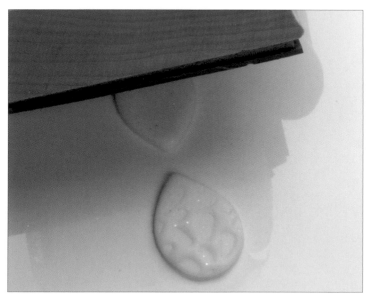

2   Stamp the wings with a dot-patterned rubber stamp.

Opposite:

The fun little mushrooms on the tag are easy to make using the same techniques as for the card itself.

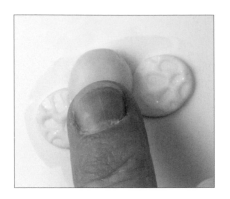

3 Roll a 1cm (⅜in) diameter ball of flesh coloured clay. Flatten it slightly and press it between the two wings.

4 Roll a tiny ball of clay for the nose and press it on to the middle of the ball. Use the embossing tool to create the eyes and the mouth.

5 Roll a small sausage of green clay for the body, 1.5cm (½in) thick. Flatten it slightly and cut across the end. Press this under the head.

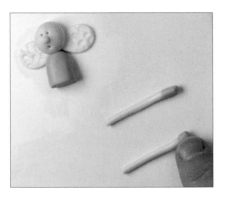

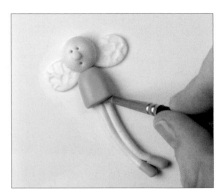

6 Roll a long thin sausage of flesh-coloured clay. Cut two 2cm (¾in) lengths for the arms and two 3.5cm (1½in) lengths for the legs.

7 Add a small ball of green clay to the end of each leg. Roll the clay to attach the ball.

8 Press the legs into the green body using the clay shaper to help.

9 Press the scroll-patterned rubber stamp on to a 3cm (1¼in) sausage of orange clay. Press this under the body, across the top of the legs to create the skirt.

10 Press the arms into place.

11 Cut eight small orange flowers using the cutter and use the embossing tool to create the flower centres.

12 Press one flower on to each foot, one where the hands meet and arrange the remaining five flowers round the fairy's head. Bake your fairy on the ceramic tile following the manufacturer's instructions.

13 Use strong clear glue to attach the patterned glitter card to the base card and attach the strip of yellow card to the middle with sticky pads.

Tip

It is a good idea to either bake your fairy right away or cover her as soon as you have finished making her. If left uncovered in her soft state, she will attract dust particles.

14 Glue the finished fairy to the yellow card.

Fun Fairy is enchanted with her ladybird surround.

Head Fairy

Just the clay head and wings of the fairy are used in this colourful card. These are pressed on to a cut-out clay flower which is stamped with the swirl motif. Bright, coordinating papers and card are used to surround our flighty friend!

Swooping Fairy

This fairy is having great fun swooping over the front of the card. She is backed with a large flower cut from background paper which is decorated with pastel flower sequins. A spotted pink paper border continues the fun element. The gift tag uses clay toadstools in matching colours as its theme.

Frivolous Fairy

Vibrantly-coloured clays are used to create this fun fairy. The base card decoration uses panels of card and background papers to reflect the colours of the clay. Small buttons are added for that funky look. The matching gift tag uses a cut out clay heart stamped with the swirl pattern and decorated with small clay flowers.

Forest Fairy

There are some beautiful rubber stamps on the market. Take time to find your perfect fairy stamp. Simply stamped and gently coloured, the Forest Fairy drifts gently within her painted and embossed panels. A torn handmade paper surround reminds her of her woodland home.

1   Paint the two pieces of thick card with jade paint. When dry, add random streaks of pale green and brown paint.

2   When dry, stamp the larger piece of card with scroll patterns using the scroll rubber stamp and an embossing pad.

3   Place it on to a sheet of scrap paper and sprinkle it with gold embossing powder. Shake off the excess powder on to the paper.

Opposite:

The tag is made with the same techniques as the card, using a Funstamps F-C18 eight pointed star rubber stamp.

4   Heat the scroll pattern with a heat tool until the powder melts and looks metallic.

YOU WILL NEED

2 pieces of thick card:
  6 x 13cm (2⅜ x 5in) and
  4 x 9.5cm (1½ x 3¾in)

Gold card 18 x 22cm (7 x 8¾in)

Green card 7 x 14cm (2¾ x 5½in)

Green handmade paper 18 x 11cm
  (7 x 4⅜in)

Acrylic paints: pale green, jade green
  and brown

Fairy rubber stamp:
  Personal Impressions P735G

Scroll pattern rubber stamp:
  Penny Black 2636K

Black inkpad

Embossing pad and gold
  embossing powder

Heat tool

Small green sequin stars

Coloured pencils – pale green, blue
  and flesh coloured

Paintbrush

Spray glue

Scrap paper

Strong clear glue

Crafter's glue

5   Use a black inkpad to stamp a fairy on to the smaller piece of painted card and leave until dry.

6   Colour the stamped fairy with coloured pencils.

7   Glue the fairy panel on top of the painted scroll panel with clear glue.

8   Decorate the area around the fairy with sequin stars, securing them with crafter's glue and moving them into place with the paintbrush.

9   Tear a 5mm (¼in) strip from each edge of the green handmade paper.

10   Score and fold the gold card down the middle and spray glue the handmade paper to the centre.

11 Glue the green card on top, again using spray glue; then attach the scroll and fairy panels to the middle of the green card with clear glue.

Fragile Forest Fairy makes the perfect centrepiece for this delicate card.

Music Fairy

Sing along with your Music Fairy (the stamp is Personal Impressions P224F) as she rests gently in her pastel world. A music stamp (Personal Impressions P593R) is used as the back panel. Sequin stars are used to cascade across the finished card. The matching gift tag has a stamp-embossed star (Funstamps F-C18) as its central motif.

Nightshade Fairy

Blue and green paints and papers are used to create this night-loving fairy (the image is Personal Impressions P736G). The same techniques are used as in the project, substituting a script rubber stamp (Sirius Hobby Stamp 'Tekst') for the back panel. Small purple stars decorate her as she drifts through the twilight.

Dancing Fairy

Cream, lilac and pink paints are used to paint the backing panels giving this fairy (made using Personal Impressions P243E) a perfect stage on which to perform her magic. The base card uses pastel colours with small pink and silver stars for decoration. The back panel uses the same stamp (Sirius Hobby Stamp 'Tekst') as the Nightshade Fairy.

Frost Fairy

Set this Frost Fairy free! Metal embossing is a wonderfully creative craft and very easy to do. Silver embossing foil and sparkling glitter are used to evoke her icy world. She is backed with starry background paper and strewn with gold stars to complete her enchanted theme.

The template for the Frost Fairy card, reproduced at actual size.

Opposite:
The finished card. Create the matching gift tag with the smaller embossed floral design.

YOU WILL NEED

Blue base card measuring 12 x 17cm (4¾ x 6¾in) when folded

Star background paper 11 x 16cm (4⁴/₁₂ x 6½in)

Grey card 9 x 14cm (3½ x 5½in)

Silver embossing foil 11 x 16cm (4⁴/₁₂ x 6½in)

Vitrail clear gloss glass-painting varnish

Small gold sequin stars

Pale blue ultra-fine glitter

Old ballpoint pen

Old scissors

Pad of paper

Paintbrush and large soft paintbrush

Crafter's glue

Strong clear glue

Scrap paper

Masking tape

The template for the Frost Fairy tag, reproduced at actual size.

41

1 Use crafter's glue to attach the star background paper to the base card and the grey card panel on top.

2 Place the foil, face down, on to a pad of paper and tape the template on top with masking tape.

3 Use a ballpoint pen to trace over the design, pressing firmly.

Tip
All the embossing work is done on the back of the foil. Turn the foil over to the front now and again to check that you have not missed any of the lines.

4 Remove the template and trace over the lines once more to deepen the embossed line.

5 Cut out the design with scissors.

6 Apply strong glue to the back and press it on to the grey card panel, smoothing it flat with your fingers.

7 Paint the background areas generously with varnish.

8 Working over a piece of scrap paper, sprinkle glitter over the wet varnish.

Tip
Shake the excess glitter on to the scrap paper, then fold the paper and pour the excess glitter back into the pot.

9 Use a large soft brush to remove excess glitter (see inset), then decorate the glitter background with stars, attaching them with crafter's glue.

The Frost Fairy is now ready to fly off into her frozen world.

Heart Fairy

Watch this silver fairy twinkle as she flies across the pink glitter card. The vibrancy is reflected in the choice of colours used for the base card, background paper and ribbon, giving this card a modern fun twist. Embossed silver mushrooms are used for the matching gift tag.

Midnight Fairy

This gleaming gold embossed fairy flashes across her starlit sky in a haze of dark blue glitter. All the elements used are gold, a real card to treasure!

Golden Fairy

Using the same techniques as for the project, gold foil and silver glitter are used to create this card. Our glistening Golden Fairy is backed with star background paper and decorated with small gold sequins. The mushroom gift tag uses the same materials – a perfect match for this enchanting card.

Templates

All of the templates on these pages are reproduced at full size except where noted.

Templates for the Fairy Queen card and tag on page 26, reproduced at three quarters of the actual size. You will need to photocopy them at 133 per cent for the correct size.

Templates for the Love Fairy card and tag on page 27.

Template for the Toadstool Fairy card on page 27, reproduced at three quarters of the actual size. You will need to photocopy it at 133 per cent for the correct size.

Templates for the Golden Fairy card
and tag on page 45.

Templates for the Heart Fairy
card and tag on page 44.

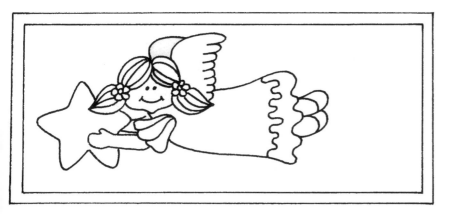

Template for the Star Fairy card on page 48.

Template for the Midnight Fairy card on page 45.

Index

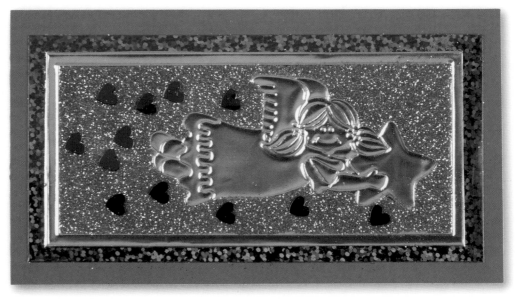

Star Fairy

Finally, this happy fairy sends you love and good wishes as she says goodbye and returns to her fairy friends. She hopes that you have found the magic while creating the cards made in her enchanted world.